Liberty and Justice for All

Prayers of Reassurance in a Time of Uncertainty

———————

Gloria Brintnall

Liberty and Justice for All-Prayers of Reassurance in a Time of Uncertainty

ISBN: 9798391135685

TABLE OF CONTENTS

FOREWORD

For over 35 years my family and I have been personally blessed by the friendship and the life-giving message of hope that Gloria lives and breathes. I can't think of a better time than now to release a book of this nature. *Liberty and Justice for All-Prayers of Reassurance in a Time of Uncertainty,* is a must read for anyone with a passion to see true justice realized in our day. This book is not only filled with history about Liberty and Justice, but it is saturated with practical hope filled prayers for a better future. Read this book; you'll never be the same.

Andrew Cunningham

Chaplain, AZ GOP 2019-2023

Pastor, Southgate Church, Phoenix, AZ

PREFACE

There was a time when I had no personal interaction with the legal/justice system of the United States. I assumed what I'd been taught in school was the truth: our judicial system was supposedly blind to bias.

I believed Lady Justice wore a blindfold because she only considered the evidence and written laws of our nation, not the ethnicity, influence, or social status of the plaintiff or defendant. As you'll soon read, the blindfold on Lady Justice doesn't represent fairness at all!

I thought perhaps my knowledge of our justice system was skewed by a few individual cases with which I was personally involved. But when our country started enforcing obviously unconstitutional mandates restricting personal liberty and expression in 2020, I began to dig a little more deeply, and what I found was frightening. Our legal system has never been completely fair. There's always been two tiers of justice. Most recently, the bottom tier of justice was for those with biblical values, including elderly Christians who were silently praying at abortion clinics who have been incarcerated for peaceful protests. On the other side of the scales of justice, members of far-left groups, who have burned cities, injured law enforcement officers, and destroyed personal property suffered few or no repercussions.

The purpose of this narrative is not to expose injustices in our legal and justice system. Most media hide the truth, but you can find it if you look. When I looked, I became terribly discouraged. I wrote emails to elected representatives to no avail.

The injustices continued. Instead of throwing up my hands and accepting the degradation of justice, I appealed to a Higher Power-the Highest Power there is- God Almighty!

I knew God was righteous and just. I also knew He was pro-liberty. But until I did a deliberate study on the subjects, I had no idea how many times the Bible addresses them. God wants liberty and justice for all. It's up to us to get in agreement with His will and ask Him to intervene in our nation. We do that by praying and declaring His Word.

Maybe you're not a religious person but you can sense that something is terribly wrong in our world today. You may not be a churchgoer, but you know right from wrong, and you've seen too many instances of evil labeled as good and good called evil. Why not try talking to God instead of complaining and cursing every time you scroll through your social media feeds?

The world may say you're an underdog. It might seem as if evil has already won and you have no chance of changing things, but with God, all things are possible.

INTRODUCTION

You probably know where we get the phrase, *with liberty and justice for all.* Most Americans grew up saying it every day in school. Some organizations still begin their meetings or assemblies with one of America's best-known pieces of prose. We call it *The Pledge of Allegiance.*

I pledge allegiance to the flag of the United States of America, and to the republic for which it stands, one nation under God, indivisible, with liberty and justice for all.

The *Pledge of Allegiance* was first released in 1892 by a Christian minister, Reverend Francis Bellamy. His original version was shorter and lacked specificity. It read, *"I pledge allegiance to my Flag and the Republic, for which it stands,—one nation, indivisible—with liberty and justice for all."*

Reverend Bellamy didn't specify to what flag or republic the pledge was addressed. Would the great numbers of *huddled masses yearning to breathe free* that found their way to America's shores consider America's flag to be *their* flag or would the phrase, *my flag,* in Bellamy's first draft, remind them of their homeland?

So, in the early 1920s, the Daughters of the American Revolution, along with some other organizations, suggested the *Pledge* be changed. A new version was adopted in 1924, which changed **my flag** to **the flag of the United States of America.**

The 1924 version read, *I pledge allegiance to the Flag of the United States of America and to the Republic for which it stands, —one nation, indivisible—with liberty and justice for all.*

A final edit to the pledge came in 1954. President Dwight D. Eisenhower asked the Congress to add the words, *under God.* He felt the addition was imperative to *"reaffirm the transcendence of religious faith in America's heritage and future and it would strengthen those spiritual weapons which forever will be our country's most powerful resource in peace and war."*

The current edition of the *Pledge of Allegiance* was agreed upon by a joint resolution of the House and Senate on Flag Day, June 14, 1954.

CHAPTER ONE

BLIND JUSTICE

Lady Justice is not a uniquely American symbol. You can find statues of the female personification of the ideal in and around courthouses, law schools, and legal and governmental buildings throughout the world. The Romans goddess, Justicia, was elevated by the emperor Augustus (27 BC-14 AD) in the pantheon and held up as a representation of one virtue Augustus hoped his leadership would promote. The massive influence of the Roman Empire carried the image of Lady Justice to nearly every continent, and she still stands today in courts, law schools and offices, and government buildings throughout the world.

Symbolic Meanings of Lady Justice's Accessories

Artistic representations of Lady Justice vary. Sometimes she is standing; other times she is seated. Always adorned in a Greco-Roman toga, symbolizing the age-old philosophical admiration for justice, she sometimes holds a sword. The sword represents authority that can alter a person's life. The most common of Lady Justice's accessories is a set of scales she holds in one hand. You might think the scales represent an evenness in adjudication, but they stand for the equilibrium of actions and consequences.

Blind to What?

Beginning in the 16th Century, Lady Justice added a blindfold to her accessories. Today, we assume the blindfold means justice does not consider the person who is being judged. We think it means black, white, brown, yellow, rich, poor, famous, and common will all be judged the same, based on evidence and the law. However, when the blindfold was added to the statue, it meant the opposite.

The blindfold originally was a satirical symbol that justice was often tolerant or ignorant of legal abuses by those in power. With that in mind, we should ask, *"What is Lady Justice's blindfold doing today in America? Is it assuring equal justice under the law or is it closing its eyes to infringements of written law or preferred people who break them?"*

The Reality of Justice for All

The U.S. Constitution begins by stating one of its goals as establishing justice. It says, *We the People of the United States, in order to form a more perfect Union, establish Justice...*

Why does our Constitution use justice as its foundational principle? Perhaps it was because the founders had suffered great injustices in the colonies. Their emphasis on biblical truths, which prioritize liberty and justice, could be another reason they opened the Constitution with the promise of establishing justice. However, their view of justice was blinded by their place and time in history. Looking back, we see *liberty and justice for all* was more of a dream than a reality for our founding fathers. Still, it was a worthy dream.

When the Constitution was ratified in 1787, slavery was still an accepted part of society. Contrary to current opinion, slavery didn't begin in the colonies. Slavery goes so far back in human history that it's hard to trace its origins. However, we know Abraham (in the Bible) had slaves, and he lived around the year 2,000 BC. We also know the Romans (and the Greeks to a lesser extent) were infamous for forcing slavery upon citizens of conquered states decades before the birth of Christ.

Most of the colonists carried their acceptance of slavery from their homeland, but Pennsylvania abolished slavery in 1780, seven years before they ratified the Constitution. Still, the promise of *justice for all* didn't apply to slaves as well as others in the colonies. Free men enjoyed liberty and justice; the slaves did not, and neither did women. The fourteenth amendment to the Constitution, ratified in 1868, granted citizenship to former slaves and gave everyone born in America the right to vote except women, who finally got liberty and justice to vote in 1920.

Without going into much detail, we can see that *liberty and justice for all* in the first century of American life was more like *liberty and justice* for male landowners. America still had a long way to go to achieve *liberty and justice for all.*

Many times, in law and government, what is written is misinterpreted and thus, justice is denied. For example, although freed slaves were promised liberty and justice in 1868, blacks in America, as a whole, were not enjoying liberty and justice. So, almost one hundred years later, in 1964, the Civil Rights Act passed, which tore down the *separate but equal* fallacy prompted by Jim Crow laws. It was a step toward the promise of *liberty and justice for all,* but it was still controlled by individual courts, judges, juries, prosecuting attorneys, and defense attorneys, who could exert bias or prejudice towards or against the defendant, the plaintiff, or the state.

Racism or classism has been a detriment to justice in nearly every nation and era. I've witnessed it myself. In the early 2000s, a friend of mine couldn't sleep, so he went for a drive late at night. He was new to the east valley of Phoenix, Arizona, and just wanted to drive and explore the suburban city to which he had just moved. He stopped for gas at a self-serve station where an older white man accused my friend of threatening him. My friend is black; he's also big and strong but as peaceful and kind as any person I know. He's a firm believer in Jesus and would never threaten anyone. However, the older gentleman felt threatened, and called the police, claiming my friend tried to rob him at gunpoint. Regardless of the fact the complainant was unharmed, no gun was found anywhere in the vicinity, and my friend was minding his own business fueling his car, he spent the night in a city jail.

Prejudice Towards or Against the Defendant

True justice determines right and wrong based on principles, not persons. A person's skin color, income, political persuasions, sexual preference, or religious affiliation should never determine the outcome of a legal dispute. Since about 2020, there's been another swing in our search for *liberty and justice for all.* It can be summarized by considering two sides to a hot-topic issue and how they have been treated by our justice system.

People are passionate about abortion. Those who want it and those who oppose it see it as a pivotal issue upon which many other issues lie. Both sides take to the streets for marches supporting their cause. However, lately the two sides seem to be treated very differently under the law.

Between 2022 and 2023, thirty-four pro-life activists were arrested for "blocking access to abortion clinics." Some elderly citizens were arrested for standing on sidewalks praying under their breath. In comparison, only two people were arrested for vandalizing dozens of churches pro-life pregnancy centers. They broke windows, spray painted obscenities, and destroyed property.

Compare that to how Mark Houck, a pro-life activist, and father of seven, was treated. An FBI SWAT team arrested him at the crack of dawn. About two dozen fully armed, Kevlar vested agents, beat on his door, put him in handcuffs and said they would take him with or without a warrant. They pointed guns at him and his seven children, watching from the stairs. When his wife asked to see the warrant for his arrest, she was told, *"We don't need to show you a warrant."* They arrested him for a charge for which he had already been acquitted. His lawyer told the Department of Justice he would turn himself in, but they attacked his home as if he were an armed terrorist. Such a demonstration of government power against an unarmed, non-violent man and his family makes us question, *"Is Lady Justice blind, providing equal justice under the law or is she closing her eyes, giving justice, and mercy to only those on the far-left side of any issue?"*

Overall, America has come a long way in its quest for liberty and justice for all. This nation abolished slavery, gave women the vote, and fought for civil rights. But the attainment of *liberty and justice for all* is still an ongoing battle. Many battles are raging underneath the surface of common knowledge; most people don't even know about the inequities in our legal system until it involves them personally. The media have taken part in hiding many stories, including the validity of Hunter Biden's laptops, what happened on January 6, 2021, and how our elections are being run. As always, the fight for *liberty and justice for all* seems to be a David vs. Goliath scenario, but a young shepherd boy took down a 9 ½ foot tall giant with one smooth stone and the power of God.

CHAPTER TWO

WHEN THERE'S LIBERTY AND JUSTICE FOR SOME

We've looked at a few instances throughout the history of the United States when some, and not all citizens experienced liberty and justice. What is a legal, effective, and appropriate way to respond when you see individuals or groups getting the short end of the liberty and justice stick?

Letters, Posters, Protests, Boycotts, and Riots

Movements from Abolition to Women's Suffrage to Civil Rights have found themselves in a fight for liberty and justice. Changing laws begins with changing hearts, but that doesn't happen easily, quickly or without some degree of pain and suffering.

Contacting Legislators, Governors, and even the President of the United States is the first step many take. But when elected officials were deaf to their pleas, those who sought liberty and justice have resorted to more dramatic action.

Some bought advertising in large papers. Others made wearable clapboard signs with their messages; then they donned them and walked up and down busy city streets for hours, days, weeks, months, and years.

Gathering hundreds or thousands of people to protest in support of a cause or person has been quite effective in garnering public support for an issue. Protests have worked to motivate elected officials to change policy. Boycotts, an organized effort to stop using or buying particular products, have been effective at eliciting change. For example, the Montgomery Bus Boycott of

1955-56, finally brought liberty and justice to blacks using public transportation in that city when their boycott caused the local transportation department to run out of cash.

Riots seem to have taken center stage in recent times. Protests are legal and protected under the Constitution's First Amendment. Riots, however, are not protected. The difference is that riots are violent and destroy public or personal property. Pro-abortion groups have done serious damage to many Catholic churches and Women's Crisis Pregnancy Centers since the Supreme Court overturned Roe v. Wade, which turns the question of abortion back to the states. Still, pro-abortion pundits call those in the pro-life movement "evil women haters" who want to go back to the Dark Ages.

A Price to Pay for Being Unpopular

Those fighting for liberty and justice in the Abolition (of slavery) movement were often ostracized from society. A few were hung as traitors.

Women in the suffrage movement, many of whom were also Abolitionists, endured terrible persecution. People threw garbage and rotten eggs while shouting expletives at them and many jails treated them inhumanely.

There's a price to pay for fighting for *liberty and justice* for all.

Those who marched alongside Martin Luther King, Jr. often faced incarceration, tear gas, fire hoses and ostracization. Some lost their jobs. Today, those who fight for liberty are often banned from social media, censored on news media, and unfairly put under government scrutiny. Some lose their jobs.

Parents who spoke at School Board Meetings have been called terrorists, put on government watch lists, and some had their personal information published as a threat to their safety. But what can we do when we witness liberty and justice for some, but not for all?

The best thing we can do is appeal to the Judge of judges, our Creator and Father. We can and should pray, asking God to intervene.

We hold these truths to be self-evident, that all men are created equal, that they are endowed by their Creator with certain unalienable Rights, that among these are Life, Liberty, and the Pursuit of Happiness.

The Declaration of Independence

CHAPTER THREE

WHY PRAY?

President Eisenhower added the phrase *under God* to the *Pledge* as a reminder that God was (and is) bigger than any threat, including the threat of a powerful, determined, and nuclear enabled Soviet Union whose goal was creating a Communist Empire that would include all of North and South America. In the 1950s and 60s, fear gripped America as children practiced *duck and cover* drills in elementary school and communities and families built bomb shelters. The Russian Bear was huge, ferocious, and unwavering in their threats. Americans needed to remember that God was bigger than the Soviets or any other power that might attack.

Since Eisenhower's day, the threats against *liberty and justice for all* have changed, but God hasn't. He is *still* bigger than anything that could come against our nation, foreign or domestic.

Americans should act civically by speaking up, voting, and attending legislative, city council and school board meetings to stand for *liberty and justice for all,* but the odds are often stacked against those lofty aspirations. Therefore, as President Eisenhower entreated, today we must remember the *transcendence of religious faith*, meaning God is bigger than anyone or anything. Stop and think about that for a moment. God is bigger than the most influential person or group on earth-whether they're behind-the-scenes or on center stage. But for some reason, big and good as God is, our world is a mess.

If There is a God, Why is There So Much Evil?

If God is bigger than any person or group, and He has not checked out of this world, then why is evil so prevalent? Isn't God omnipotent? Isn't He sovereign?

Yes, God is *omnipotent*, meaning *all powerful*. He is also *sovereign*, meaning *supreme and superior*. God is big and powerful enough to take out all evildoers and destroy all wickedness, but He won't because He always keeps His promises.

After God created Adam and Eve, He gave them authority over this earth and everything in it. *Genesis 1:26* says *God said, Let us make man in our image, after our likeness: and **let them have dominion** over the fish of the sea, and over the fowl of the air, and over the cattle, and **over all the earth,** and over every creeping thing that creepeth upon the earth.*

God created humans as free moral agents. He doesn't force *anyone* to obey Him. That's why He gave Adam and Eve the ability to choose.

When Adam and Eve bowed to the serpent and eat of the tree of the knowledge of good and evil, they yielded their authority to the devil.

How can we know that is true?

First, when the devil was tempting Jesus in the wilderness, Satan said, *All this power will I give thee, and the glory of them:* ***for that is delivered unto me****; and to whomsoever I will I give it.* (Luke 4:6)

In other words, "I was just a lowly serpent in the Garden of Eden until I convinced the man and woman to believe me instead *of God. When they did, they elevated me to the one with dominion and authority. They became my servants instead of God's."*

Second, *Romans 6:16* says, *Know ye not, **that to whom ye yield yourselves servants to obey, his servants ye are to whom ye obey;** whether of sin unto death, or of obedience unto righteousness?*

Why is there so much evil in the world if God is real, alive, and just? It's because God is *not* in control on the earth unless we give Him control. There is a god of this world, but it's not the God of creation who sent His Son, Jesus, to die on the cross and rise from the grave. The *god of this world* is pure evil. *2 Corinthians 4:4* tells us one who blinds the eyes of people who don't believe in Jesus is the one running the earth. It says, *In whom **the god of this world hath blinded the minds of them which believe not**, lest the light of the glorious gospel of Christ, who is the image of God, should shine unto them.*

God is Only in Control if You Put Him in Control

This may come as a shock, but God is not in control of everything that happens on the earth. Most Christian folks say, *"Don't worry about a thing. God is in control."* But God is only in control if you put Him in control.

You might have never heard a preacher mention it, but it is very clear throughout Scripture and in the daily news. Satan is the *god of this world.*

The God of Creation is bigger than Satan, but the *god of this world* is behind hatred, addiction, crime, wars, fascism, perversion, communism, racism, wokeism, and every other *ism.* When President Eisenhower added the phrase *under God* to the *Pledge of Allegiance,* he did it to remind a frightened nation that the God of Creation was bigger than the *god of this world* who was inflaming and enraging the Russian Bear.

27

How to Get Free from the god of This World's Power

The devil runs and rules everyone who has not committed their lives to Jesus Christ. The earth is full of agony because that's all the devil does. He only comes to *steal, kill, and destroy. (John 10:10)*

Newborn babies are precious. God has a plan for every baby's life, but when they are born, as cute as they are, they are born with the sin nature.

If you've raised a child, you know you had to teach them just about everything-how to feed themselves, and how to walk, talk, and play. By the time they're about two years old, you realize they know something you never taught them. They know how to rebel! They know instinctively how to run away when you call or how to hide the cookie they weren't supposed to be eating when you came in the room!

The default setting for every person on this earth is not righteousness and life; it is sin and death. Adam sinned and the sin nature passed down to every person born of man. (That's why the Messiah had to be born of a virgin. If He had a natural father, He would have been born with the sin nature.)

Romans 5:12 confirms that every person naturally born on this earth is born as a sinner. It says, *Wherefore, as by one man sin entered into the world, and death by sin; and so death passed upon all men, for that all have sinned.*

When Adam turned his authority over to the devil, he also sold all humanity into his hands.

When Jesus died on the cross and rose from the dead, He made redemption available. Redemption is buying something back or exchanging one thing for another. The only way out from under the *god of this world's* power is through a relationship with Jesus. Redemption is available to all but forced on none.

Some people choose to stay under the evil one's thumb. They are the ones through whom he steals, kills, and destroys. But those who have accepted Jesus as the Son of God who died on the cross and rose from the dead, have appropriated His gift of redemption. Speaking of Jesus, Paul wrote, *In whom we have redemption through his blood, the forgiveness of sins, according to the riches of his grace. (Ephesians 1:7)*

Going to a nice church will not free anyone from the power of the *god of this world.* As an example, ask yourself if church-going was the way to freedom from evil, why have there been so many reports of sexual misconduct and child abuse happening within churches? It's because the *god of this world* is still directing those people.

The only way to be free from the *god of this world* is to dethrone him. Kick him out of your life and get him out of your heart by inviting Jesus to take His place in the center of your life. All you have to do is acknowledge Him as the Son of God who died on the cross and rose from the dead. Ask Him to take the center spot in your heart. He will take up residence in your spirit and give you freedom, peace, joy, and life everlasting.

Now, you are no longer under the devil's hand. You belong to God. Jesus bought back (redeemed) Adam's authority and as one of His followers, you've got it too.

When Jesus rose from the dead, He took Satan's authority. *Colossians 2:15 (NLT)* says when Jesus rose from the grave, *he disarmed the spiritual rulers and authorities. He shamed them publicly by his victory over them on the cross.*

Jesus acknowledged all power was given to Him after He rose from the dead. Then, He told His followers to *go and teach all nations.* In other words, Jesus redeemed the power God gave to Adam at creation and He makes it available to those who believe in Him.

Matthew 28:17-19 says, And when they saw him, they worshipped him: but some doubted. And Jesus came and spake unto them, saying, All power is given unto me in heaven and in earth. Go ye therefore, and teach all nations, baptizing them in the name of the Father, and of the Son, and of the Holy Ghost.

It's All About Power

God is the source of all power. The devil's M.O. is to usurp God's power. Isaiah 14 tells how Lucifer, the most honored angel in heaven, fell and became the lead demon we call the devil. It says, *How art thou fallen from heaven, O Lucifer, son of the morning! how art thou cut down to the ground, which didst weaken the nations! For thou hast said in thine heart, I will ascend into heaven, I will exalt my throne above the stars of God: I will sit also upon the mount of the congregation, in the sides of the north: I will ascend above the heights of the clouds; I will be like the most High. (Isaiah 14:12-14)*

Lucifer wanted God's position and power, and he still does. Power is a mighty motivator. Every international war and locally driven political battle is over power, and many of the battles citizens face today are rooted in the desire of governments to assume power and authority that rightly belongs to God. When governments closed churches and locked down cities because of a virus, they effectively put citizens on house arrest. People waited for the government to return their freedom to make a living, see family members and enjoy social functions. But those freedoms should never have been abdicated to the government because they came from God.

The Declaration of Independence acknowledges that our rights of life, liberty and the pursuit of happiness come from God, not the government. It says, *We hold these truths to be self-evident, that all men are created equal, that they are endowed by their Creator with certain unalienable Rights, that among these are Life, Liberty and the Pursuit of Happiness.*

When people trust the government over God, they empower the government to control them, and as the bureaucracies grow, they assert more power over their citizens. God, not government is the source of our liberty and justice. If we look to the government instead of God for freedom or righteous judgment, we give a man-made system honor that belongs to God.

John Hancock, the first man to sign the Declaration of Independence said, "*Resistance to tyranny becomes the Christian and social duty of each individual. ... Continue steadfast and, with a proper sense of your dependence on God, nobly defend those rights which heaven gave, and no man ought to take from us.*"

Thomas Jefferson, the third President, who drafted the Declaration of Independence, acknowledged God as our source of liberty when he said, "*God who gave us life gave us liberty. And can the liberties of a nation be thought secure when we have* removed their only firm basis, a conviction in the minds of the people that these liberties are of the Gift of God? That they are not to be violated but with His wrath? Indeed, I tremble for my country when I reflect that God is just; that His justice cannot sleep forever..."

Jefferson also said, *"And can the liberties of a nation be thought secure when we have removed their only firm basis, a conviction in the minds of the people that these liberties are of the gift of God? That they are not to be violated but with His wrath? Indeed I tremble for my country when I reflect that God is just; that his justice cannot sleep forever."*

As we pray, we reaffirm God's authority in our lives. We also open the door to His power that can overcome all earthly powers. When governmental powers take away our liberty and don't enforce justice, where can we go? We should reach out to the God of all creation. He is bigger than the biggest bureaucracy, wiser than the most well-known "think tank" and more powerful than any weapon of mass destruction.

Effective Prayer

God acts in response to the prayers of His people. John Wesley, the founder of the Methodist church, said, *"It seems God is limited by our prayer life. He can do nothing for humanity unless someone asks Him."*

So, stop expecting God to do something when you haven't even talked to Him about it!

CHAPTER FOUR

PRAYING FOR LIBERTY AND JUSTICE

Prayer is a two-way conversation with the Living God of the Universe. Many Christians encourage people to simply *"pour their hearts out to God."* God loves His people, and He is ready to hear every cry of your heart. However, when the disciples asked Jesus to teach them to pray, He didn't respond, *"Just pour your heart out to God."* He gave them specifics about how to address God and what to say. Many know this section of Scripture as *The Our Father* or *The Lord's Prayer.*

Breaking Down What is Known as *The Lord's Prayer*

And it came to pass, that, as he was praying in a certain place, when he ceased, one of his disciples said unto him, Lord, teach us to pray, as John also taught his disciples. And he said unto them, When ye pray, say, Our Father which art in heaven, Hallowed be thy name. Thy kingdom come. Thy will be done, as in heaven, so in earth. Give us day by day our daily bread. And forgive us our sins; for we also forgive every one that is indebted to us. And lead us not into temptation; but deliver us from evil. (Luke 11:1-4)

Jesus was not implying praying the above verses exactly by rote was the only way to pray. So, instead of looking at the prayer from *Luke 11:1-4* as the perfect script for a memorized prayer, we should approach it as the perfect outline of prayer principles.

Our Father which art in heaven- The first prayer principle is to address the Father.

Hallowed be thy name- The second prayer principle is to acknowledge that God alone is God. The word *hallowed* means *holy, venerated, or sanctified.* Declare who God is. You might use His redemptive names by saying, *"You are Jehovah Tsidkenue, my Righteousness. You are Jehovah Rophe, my Healer. You are Jehovah Shalom, my Peace. You are Jehovah Shammah, the God who is here present with me. Thank You, God, that You are Jehovah M'Kaddesh, the God who is my sanctification. You alone, God are Jehovah Jireh, my Provider. You are El Roi, the God who sees. I worship You and adore You for Who You are!* Psalm 100:4 says, *Enter into his gates with thanksgiving, and into his courts with praise: be thankful unto him, and bless his name.*

Thy Kingdom Come- This phrase can be problematic if you don't take all of Scripture into consideration. On one hand, we've already received the kingdom of God. Jesus said, *the kingdom of God is within you. (Luke 17:21)* On the other hand, *Revelation 12:10* reminds us of a day yet to come when God's kingdom will rule over the entire earth. It says, *And I heard a loud voice saying in heaven, Now is come salvation, and strength, and the kingdom of our God, and the power of his Christ: for the accuser of our brethren is cast down, which accused them before our God day and night.*

Thy will be done on earth as it is in heaven- As mentioned in Chapter Three, God's will won't happen automatically. He moves in the earth when His people ask Him. When you sincerely pray, *"Thy will be done,"* you give up your opinions and desires and submit yourself to His. Many people view prayer as a sort of holy order placing system like the drive through at Starbucks. They want to give God their "order" with great specifics. Prayer is a way to open the door for God to move and have His way. It's not meant to be a tool for you to have yours.

Jesus said we should pray for God's will to be manifested on the earth as it is in heaven. So, if you wonder how to pray about a situation, ask yourself, *"how is this in heaven?"* There's no sickness, lack, suffering, evil, depravity or pain in heaven. So, you should pray accordingly. Don't pray for the strength to put up with sickness, lack, suffering, evil, depravity or pain. Pray to be free of it!

Give us this day our daily bread- God is your provider and there's nothing wrong with praying for your natural needs. However, this kind of prayer should be prayed by faith, noting that God's Word promises to meet his children's needs. In your prayer, include some Scriptures that promise God's provision and tell Him you are standing on His Word, and you know He always keeps His Word. Then, give Him thanks it is so!

And forgive us our sins; for we also forgive every one that is indebted to us- Christians can and do sin, so we need to repent when we do, get forgiven and move forward! *1 John 1:9* says *if we confess our sins, he is faithful and just to forgive us our sins, and to cleanse us from all unrighteousness.*

If you want your prayers to be effective, you need to be forgiven and you also need to forgive. Unforgiveness hinders prayers. In *Mark 11:24-26* Jesus said, *Therefore I say unto you,*

What things soever ye desire, when ye pray, believe that ye receive them, and ye shall have them. And when ye stand praying, forgive, if ye have ought against any: that your Father also which is in heaven may forgive you your trespasses. But if ye do not forgive, neither will your Father which is in heaven forgive your trespasses.

You don't have to feel happy about what happened, nor do you have to have warm fuzzies towards those who hurt you. Just forgive. Release the offense and let God handle it. After all, He is the God of justice!

And lead us not into temptation; but deliver us from evil- This is another challenging section of the prayer, but if you look at it in the context of other Scripture, you'll see what Jesus meant.

First, God does not lead people into temptation. *James 1:13* says, *let no man say when he is tempted, I am tempted of God: for God cannot be tempted with evil, neither tempteth he any man.* Let's turn it around. Instead of praying what we *don't* want to be led into, perhaps we should pray about what we want to be led into. Instead of, *"Lord, lead us not into temptation,"* we should pray that we are led by the Holy Spirit, according to *Romans 8:14*, which says, *For as many as are led by the Spirit of God, they are the sons of God.*

Second, *Colossians 1:13* says Jesus has already delivered us from the evil one. It says, *who hath delivered us from the power of darkness, and hath translated us into the kingdom of his dear Son.* But when Jesus taught His disciples to pray, He hadn't died on the cross or risen from the dead. Their position wasn't the same as ours! New Testament believers have been delivered and we should thank God for it every time we pray.

Effective Praying

Jesus taught His disciples to pray according to their spiritual state. He had not conquered sin and death yet; that's why some of the *Lord's Prayer* prays for things Jesus has already provided for us in His death and resurrection. The Bible has many verses about prayer. Some, particularly in the book of Psalms, are a pouring out of one's heart. Others, especially in the New Testament, give us specific instructions about how to pray effectively. *James 5:16* says, *the effectual fervent prayer of a righteous man availeth much.* If some prayers can be effectual, then that must mean some prayers can be ineffectual. You may feel better after simply complaining or crying to God, but that probably won't stir up enough power to change you or your situation.

Although the Bible has hundreds of verses about prayer, I want to share only two that, when followed, will turn your prayers into effective, mobilizing action that happens first in the spiritual realm, but will always eventually manifest in the natural realm.

1 John 5:14-15 is what I call God's *prayer guarantee.* It says, *and this is the confidence that we have in him, that, if we ask any thing according to his will, he heareth us: And if we know that he hear us, whatsoever we ask, we know that we have the petitions that we desired of him.*

Please stop and read *1 John 5:14-15* again...slowly. If we ask anything according to His will, He hears us and we know if He hears us, we have the petitions we ask of Him!

If you want your prayers answered, be sure they agree with God's will. How can you know God's will? His Word is His will, so when you pray God's Word, you can know that it will come to pass.

Jesus said, *if ye abide in me, and my words abide in you, ye shall ask what ye will, and it shall be done unto you. (John 15:7)*

The rest of this book will be primarily God's Word about liberty and justice. Meditate on His Word and pray them aloud. Pray them in faith and then believe things are moving in God's direction, and give Him thanks that it is done!

Liberty and Justice

The words *liberty* and *justice* are not only political words; they are Bible words.

Liberty is *personal freedom* and, although many don't understand this, God is all about personal freedom. He set the tree in the middle of the Garden of Eden so the first man and woman could choose to obey (or disobey) His command to not eat of it. God forces no one to do what is right. He does, however enforce justice and judgment because they are the foundation of Who He is. *Psalm 89:14* says, *justice and judgment are the habitation of thy throne: mercy and truth shall go before thy face.*

Let's pray God's Word to bring liberty and justice for all. As you read the following Scriptures, pray them. Change the pronouns as needed and add certain specifics when appropriate. For example, you could *turn Psalm 89:14* into a prayer by saying: *"Father God, justice and judgment are the habitation of Your throne. I'm asking that You enforce justice and judgment in the case of (fill in the blanks). Mercy and truth go before Your face, O God. Send mercy to those who will respond to Your great kindness but let truth be exposed however it needs to be done, in Jesus' name. Amen!"*

Resistance to tyranny becomes the Christian and social duty of each individual. ... Continue steadfast and, with a proper sense of your dependence on God, nobly defend those rights which heaven gave, and no man ought to take from us.

John Hancock

CHAPTER FIVE

PRAYING THE BIBLE WAY ABOUT LIBERTY

Since God's Word is His will, and He said He would hear and answer prayers that are according to His will (*1 John 5:14-15*), we're going to explore Bible verses about liberty and justice, then we will pray according to those Scriptures. Let's begin with a few Bible verses about liberty.

The Citation on the Liberty Bell

Leviticus 25:10 (the inscription on the Liberty Bell was taken directly from this Scripture.) *And ye shall hallow the fiftieth year, and proclaim liberty throughout all the land unto all the inhabitants thereof: it shall be a jubilee unto you; and ye shall return every man unto his possession, and ye shall return every man unto his family.*

You can pray this verse like this: God of all creation, You set Your people in their land to live as free men and women. You told them to proclaim liberty to everyone in the land. So, Lord, we proclaim liberty throughout our nation. We say, this is a land of freedom for all, in Jesus' name.

More Verses About Liberty

Psalm 119: 45 says, *I will walk at liberty: for I seek thy precepts.*

Pray: God, You are the source of freedom, and I seek Your ways so I can live in liberty. You give us liberty to live for You, not so we can live in sin. I pray for our nation and ask that more people would seek Your precepts so they can walk in true liberty.

Isaiah 61:1-2 *The Spirit of the Lord God is upon me; because the Lord hath anointed me to preach good tidings unto the meek; he hath sent me to bind up the brokenhearted, to proclaim liberty to the captives, and the opening of the prison to them that are bound; To proclaim the acceptable year of the Lord, and the day of vengeance of our God; to comfort all that mourn.*

Pray: Father, You have anointed Your people to proclaim liberty to captives. Some people are captive to addictions. Others are captive to reliance on government; still others are captive to what people think about them. As one of Your anointed children, I proclaim liberty! I speak freedom over people who are captive to addictions, other people's opinions, or government injustice. I declare freedom to those who were unjustly convicted of crimes and wrongly incarcerated. Protect them, Lord, and set them free! I proclaim liberty by the anointing of the Holy Spirit, in Jesus' name.

Jeremiah 34:15 *And ye were now turned, and had done right in my sight, in proclaiming liberty every man to his neighbour; and ye had made a covenant before me in the house which is called by my name.*

Pray: Father, we remind You of the covenant the settlers made with You when they landed on Virginia Beach in 1607. They dedicated themselves and this land to You, Lord. When they planted a roughly hewn wooden cross in the sands of Virginia Beach, they declared their purpose was *"to reach the people within these shores with the Gospel of Jesus Christ, and to raise up Godly generations after us, and with these generations take the Kingdom of God to all the earth."* Their Covenant was *"for all generations, as long as the earth remains,"* so, Lord, we call upon that covenant. We reaffirm this nation is here to spread the Gospel and to do that, we need liberty! We need to be free to do what You tell us to do without government interference. Remember Your covenant with the early settlers of this land so we may fulfill our part, in Jesus' mighty name!

Romans 8:20-22 *For the creature was made subject to vanity, not willingly, but by reason of him who hath subjected the same in hope, Because the creature itself also shall be delivered from the bondage of corruption into the glorious liberty of the children of God. For we know that the whole creation groaneth and travaileth in pain together until now.*

Pray: Oh God, the earth is groaning from the burden of sin, but as Your people, we are grateful to have been delivered from the bondage and corruption the devil has wrought on this earth. Thank You, Lord, that we live in glorious liberty as Your children. We are spiritually free from sin, but we acknowledge we're not always free as citizens. Father, we ask that You do whatever is needed to keep Your people free to serve You, to raise their families according to Your Word, and to share the Gospel in public places. All of creation is groaning for the spiritual freedom You've provided for us in Christ. Help us to boldly share Your Truth and Your love to a hurting world, in Jesus' name.

2 Corinthians 3:17 *Now the Lord is that Spirit: and where the Spirit of the Lord is, there is liberty.*

Pray: Father, we open the door to our homes, our government, our churches, our businesses, our schools, our marketplaces, our health care facilities, our highways, and our hearts to Your Holy Spirit. He does not bring condemnation, but conviction. He is our Comforter, our Helper, and our Intercessor. His presence brings peace, power, and possibilities. We pray especially for local churches to experience true freedom by Your Holy Spirit. We know You do things decently and in order, and when the Holy Spirit runs a church service, people are free to hear clearly from Your Word. The sick are healed; the lost find their way with You; those whose lives are a wandering generality find focus and purpose. Let Your Spirit flow and bring true liberty to fulfill Your purpose throughout this land, in Jesus' name.

Galatians 3:4 *And that because of false brethren unawares brought in, who came in privily to spy out our liberty which we have in Christ Jesus, that they might bring us into bondage.*

Pray: Dear Father, we are so thankful for our relationship with You through Jesus. Over the centuries, religions have tried to restrict people's freedoms. Even today, some religions add things You never did to the Gospel. But when Your people have been conditioned to live as subservient to other people (even in church), they too easily fall into allowing the government to rule their lives. God, let Your people understand the beauty and the responsibility of our freedom in Christ, and help them mature as believers, knowing what is of You and what is not, in Jesus' name.

Galatians 5:1: *Stand fast therefore in the liberty wherewith Christ hath made us free, and be not entangled again with the yoke of bondage.*

Pray: God, You could have created us to be little robots, always obedient to Your commands, but You didn't! You love freedom so much that You sent Jesus to die on the cross to set us free from the tyranny of the devil. Thank You for freedom in Jesus!

Galatians 5:13: *For, brethren, ye have been called unto liberty; only use not liberty for an occasion to the flesh, but by love serve one another.*

Pray: Abba, Father, we don't want to act like out-of-control children with the freedom You've given us. We haven't seen anyone drop dead because they lied like Ananias and Sapphira did in the fifth chapter of Acts, so we sometimes get a little lax in our behavior and attitude. Still, we know one day, we will be rewarded for doing what You told us to do. We repent for using our freedom and our prosperity for purely selfish reasons. We commit to use our freedom to live holy lives and help others enjoy liberty and fulfillment in Christ.

James 1:25 *But whoso looketh into the perfect law of liberty, and continueth therein, he being not a forgetful hearer, but a doer of the work, this man shall be blessed in his deed.*

Pray: God, Thank You for the Constitution of the United States. It was ordained of You. There is more wisdom in that document than most people know. Still, it's not the perfect law of liberty; Your Word is. Help us, Lord to look at Your Word, remember it, and do it, even when things in this world are topsy-turvy and people are calling right wrong and wrong right, in Jesus' name.

2 Peter 2:18-19 *For when they speak great swelling words of vanity, they allure through the lusts of the flesh, through much wantonness, those that were clean escaped from them who live in error. While they promise them liberty, they themselves are the servants of corruption: for of whom a man is overcome, of the same is he brought in bondage.*

Pray: Woah, God! It's like these verses of Scripture were written yesterday! I guess it's because people are people. Ever since the serpent in the Garden of Eden, Satan has known how to lie in a way that appeals to the masses, and like Eve, too many of Your people fall for the lies! Many politicians and activists today promise freedom and a better life, but there's always a catch. When we rely on government agencies instead of You, we lose freedom; we never gain it. Father, I ask that You open people's eyes to the lies they're being told. I pray people will depend on You instead of a government agency, and that the church of the Lord Jesus Christ will arise to help in times of need, so people don't have to rely on the government. In Jesus' name.

CHAPTER SIX

PRAYING THE BIBLE WAY ABOUT JUSTICE

Webster's 1828 dictionary says *justice* is *the virtue which consists in giving to every one what is his due;* practical conformity to the laws and to principles of rectitude in the dealings of men with each other; honesty.

God is just. He will forgive anyone who confesses and repents of any sin. Jesus died for everyone-the rich and influential or the poor and downtrodden. God's laws work for everyone who works them; they even work for those who don't believe in Him. For example, the idea of *karma* or *the law of attraction*, both touted by people who don't believe in Jesus, work because they are a manifestation of God's law of sowing and reaping. God's laws work for everyone if they work them.

Similarly, God's judgment is based on one thing alone: what did you do with my Son, Jesus Christ? Did you accept His sacrifice on the cross for your sins? Did you believe He rose from the dead? Did you pray to make Him your Savior and Lord? One hundred percent of people who do those things will be born-again. They will all go to heaven when they die. The rich don't get a better or easier way. The poor don't have to stand to the side and watch. God's judgment is completely fair because He is a God of justice.

Jesus told us to pray God's will on earth as it is in heaven. Therefore, we should pray for justice on this earth and, as mentioned earlier, the most effective prayers come from the Bible.

The King James Bible often uses the word *judge* when speaking of *justice*. In the following verses, if the King James is not clear in its reference to justice, I've added more contemporary language in brackets for clarity.

Verses and Prayers about Justice

Genesis 18:19: *For I know him, that he will command his children and his household after him, and they shall keep the way of the Lord, to do justice and judgment; that the Lord may bring upon Abraham that which he hath spoken of him.*

Pray: Abba, Father, justice pleases You. Since justice pleases You, I know injustice displeases You. Lord, if there are positions I've taken personally or professionally that have not been just or fair, I repent. Show me how to be fair in every decision so I can reflect Your goodness. In Jesus' name.

Genesis 49:16-17: *Dan shall judge* [provide justice for] *his people, as one tribe of Israel. Dan shall be a serpent by the way, an adder in the path, that biteth the horse heels, so that his rider shall fall backward.*

Pray: Dear God, I ask for justice in our country that will bite the heels of those who do evil. Bite the heels of those who call evil good and good evil. Stop the propagation of immorality, bribes, immoral lawsuits, and unjust judicial decisions. Let Your justice bite the heels of those who do wrong with impunity, in Jesus' name.

Exodus 23:2-3: *Thou shalt not follow a multitude to do evil; neither shalt thou speak in a cause to decline after many to wrest judgment* [when you give testimony in a lawsuit, do not pervert justice by siding with the crowd]*: Neither shalt thou countenance a poor man in his cause* [do not show favoritism to a poor man in his lawsuit].

Pray: Lord, I'm sorry for the times I've followed the crowd instead of You. Help me hear from You and empower me with boldness to stand alone for what is right if that's the way it needs to be. God, I pray for our country. I ask that people would stop falling for lies that incite anger, strife, and hatred. Open their eyes, Lord. Give them a desire to do what's right, not what's popular, in Jesus' name.

Leviticus 19:15: *Ye shall do no unrighteousness in judgment* [Do not pervert justice]*: thou shalt not respect the person of the poor* [Do not show partiality to the poor]*, nor honor the person of the mighty* [or favoritism to the great]*: but in righteousness shalt thou judge thy neighbour* [judge your neighbor fairly].

Pray: God, I pray that our judges, juries, lawyers, elected officials, and bureaucrats would stop perverting justice! We pray honest people would no longer be weighed down and choked by lawfare. God, hear us as we petition You! Set the innocent free and bring the guilty to trial, in Jesus' name!

Deuteronomy 16:19-20: *Thou shalt not wrest judgment; thou shalt not respect persons* [Do not pervert justice or show partiality], *neither take a gift: for a gift doth blind the eyes of the wise, and pervert the words of the righteous.* [Do not accept a bribe.]

Pray: Father, in the name of Jesus, I ask that any elected official of any party that has taken bribes would be exposed and stopped. God, You know who's taking bribes, who paid them, and what for. You know how to stop them, and I ask You to stop bribery in our city, state, and our nation.

Deuteronomy 33:20-21(Moses, blessing the Tribes of Israel, here, he speaks of Gad):

And of Gad he said, Blessed be he that enlargeth Gad: he dwelleth as a lion, and teareth the arm with the crown of the head. And he provided the first part for himself, because there, in a portion of the lawgiver, was he seated; and he came with the heads of the people, he executed the justice of the Lord, and his judgments with Israel.

Pray: Father, I pray for those who are just judges in our land. Protect them. Provide for them. Give them wisdom and favor. Command Your angels concerning them to guard them so they can continue to judge righteously. Bless them with promotion and favor with the public. Let their righteous judgments be an example to others, and help more to judge justly, in Jesus' name!

1 Samuel 8:1-3: *And it came to pass, when Samuel was old, that he made his sons judges over Israel. Now the name of his* *firstborn was Joel; and the name of his second, Abiah: they were judges in Beersheba. And his sons walked not in his ways, but turned aside after lucre, and took bribes, and perverted judgment.* [They turned aside after dishonest gain, accepted bribes and perverted justice.]

Pray: God, bribery is nothing new, is it? But it's never been right. Your Word mentions it as wrong in several places. Father, there are many people who justify taking bribes by saying, *"everyone does it. I might as well raise my family's standard of living."* But they know better. They don't know, however, the long-term effects of doing things against Your Word. I pray their eyes open, and their hearts soften to do what is right; to stop taking bribes and stop acting like they're righteous when they're not! We get in agreement with Your Word, and we command those *principalities, powers, rulers of the darkness of this world, and spiritual wickedness in high places (Ephesians 6:12)* to loose those giving and taking bribes so they will no longer be empowered and enriched to do wrong, in Jesus' name.

2 Samuel 8:15: *And David reigned over all Israel; and David executed judgment and justice unto all his people.*

Pray: Father, we ask for elected officials, including District Attorneys, Attorneys General, Judges, and Lawyers to execute justice, in Jesus' name!

2 Samuel 15:1-6 *And it came to pass after this, that Absalom prepared him chariots and horses, and fifty men to run before him. And Absalom rose up early, and stood beside the way of the gate: and it was so, that when any man that had a controversy came to the king for judgment, then Absalom called* *unto him, and said, Of what city art thou? And he said, Thy servant is of one of the tribes of Israel. And Absalom said unto him, See, thy matters are good and right; but there is no man deputed of the king to hear thee. Absalom said moreover, Oh that I were made judge in the land, that every man which hath any suit or cause might come unto me, and I would do him justice! And it was so, that when any man came nigh to him to do him obeisance, he put forth his hand, and took him, and kissed him. And on this manner did Absalom to all Israel that came to the king for judgment: so Absalom stole the hearts of the men of Israel.*

Pray: Wow, God! Politicians who lie to gain favor with the people are nothing new! Absalom, the King's own son, acted like he really cared for the people while he dissed his father's ability to rule the people justly and fairly. Father, why do people fall for these tricks? Why can't they see that politicians do and say things only to garner votes? Why do they join themselves to politicians who do nothing but identify with a person's race, sexual identity, income, or hometown? Father, I pray, in Jesus' name, that You wake people up! Let them see the political lies and untruths that they're being fed. And, Lord, make them bold enough to step away from a group or person who operates by lies and half-truths.

1 Kings 3:28: *And all Israel heard of the judgment which the king had judged; and they feared the king: for they saw that the wisdom of God was in him, to do judgment* [he had wisdom from God to administer justice].

Pray: Father, in the name of Jesus, I ask that You give us judges who fear You and who will seek wisdom and do justice!

1 Kings 10:9 and 2 Chronicles 9:8: *Blessed be the Lord thy God, which delighted in thee, to set thee on the throne of Israel: because the Lord loved Israel for ever, therefore made he thee king, to do judgment and justice.*

Pray: Father, I don't think many of our leaders have delighted You as King Solomon did. He started his reign with a right heart to obey You, but he got involved with women who didn't know or serve You, and they drew him away from You and Your ways. Father, help us find and elect government officials who delight You-who make You happy-not because they're perfect. Nobody is perfect except You, God! But help us choose leaders whose hearts are honest and righteous, in Jesus' name.

Ezra 7:25: *And thou, Ezra, after the wisdom of thy God, that is in thine hand, set magistrates and judges, which may judge all the people that are beyond the river, all such as know the laws of thy God; and teach ye them that know them not.* [Ezra, used wisdom from God to choose just judges who will rule according to God's law.]

Pray: Oh, God! Please, please give this nation wisdom to choose just judges and officials. In Jesus' name!

Job 8:3: *Doth God pervert judgment? or doth the Almighty pervert justice?*

Pray: Father, You would never pervert justice. Please forgive us for thinking You let things slide because of Your love. Your love endures forever, and Your mercies are new every morning, but You judge the living and the dead fairly-always

53

according to Your Word and always in absolute justice. I love You and thank You for Your mercy and justice, in Jesus' name!

Job 9:24: *The earth is given into the hand of the wicked: he covereth the faces of the judges thereof; if not, where, and who is he?* [When a land falls into the hands of the wicked, he blindfolds its judges. If it is not he, then who is it?]

Pray: Oh, God! It seems like this has happened to our land! It has fallen into the hands of the wicked and our judges have been blindfolded. In the name of Jesus, I repent on behalf of our nation! Your people didn't stand up for Your Word. We didn't confront evil, and we often went along with it. Sometimes we didn't know any better but sometimes we just didn't want to stand up for Your truth. Father, I ask that this nation be freed from the hands of the wicked and the blindfolds come off the eyes of judges, in Jesus' name. Amen.

Job 34:12: *Yea, surely God will not do wickedly, neither will the Almighty pervert judgment* [justice].

Pray: Father, You never do evil and You never pervert justice. You are love. You are good. You are holy. You are just. You are righteous. You are awesome and today I completely put my trust in You, in Jesus' name.

Job 34:17: *Shall even he that hateth right govern? and wilt thou condemn him that is most just?* [Can he who hates justice rule?]

Pray: Lord, it seems like we have some people in positions of power who hate justice. They want to use our judicial system to persecute their political opponents. God, that is not of You and I take authority over that and command it to stop, in Jesus' name. I will stand on Your Word as long as it takes because faith and patience inherit your promises. You are bigger than any person or group and I call upon You to save our nation, in Jesus' name.

Job 34:20-24: *In a moment shall they die, and the people shall be troubled at midnight, and pass away: and the mighty shall be taken away without hand. For his eyes are upon the ways of man, and he seeth all his goings. There is no darkness, nor shadow of death, where the workers of iniquity may hide themselves. For he will not lay upon man more than right; that he should enter into judgment with God. He shall break in pieces mighty men without number, and sets others in their stead. [Without inquiry, he shatters the mighty and sets up others in their place.*

Pray: Well, Lord. I know you don't want me to pray death upon people, but this section of the book of Job is still in the Bible! It was something one of Job's friends said, and their theology wasn't necessarily one hundred percent correct. Still, God, Your Word says *vengeance is mine, saith the Lord. (Romans 12:19)* So, Lord, You know there are some very powerful people who have hardened their hearts toward You. They are antagonistic to You, Your Word, and Your people. *Romans 1:28* describes many of them: *And even as they did not like to retain God in their knowledge, God gave them over to a reprobate mind, to do those things which are not convenient.* You know the ones you've given over to a reprobate mind; I don't. But Lord, those whom You have given over, I ask You get them out of leadership positions. Get them out of positions of power, in Jesus' name.

Psalm 7:6: *Arise, O Lord, in thine anger, lift up thyself because of the rage of mine enemies: and awake for me to the judgment that thou hast commanded.* [Awake, my God; decree justice!]

Pray: Dear God, I ask You to arise! I lift You up in praise and adoration. You are bigger than my enemies! You are stronger than any army! You are richer than any nation! Arise, O Lord and take care of my enemies, in Jesus' name!

Psalm 7:9: *Oh let the wickedness of the wicked come to an end; but establish the just: for the righteous God trieth the hearts and reins.* [Bring an end to the violence and lies of the wicked and make the righteous secure.]

Pray: Oh God, let the wickedness of the wicked come to an end! Father, it seems as if evil has implanted itself in every institution in our nation. Father, the evil is great, but greater is He that is in me than he that is in the world. In the name of Jesus, I command angels to go forth and fight the spiritual battle in the atmosphere.

Psalm 9:7-9: *But the Lord shall endure for ever: he hath prepared his throne for judgment. And he shall judge the world in righteousness, he shall minister judgment to the people in uprightness. The Lord also will be a refuge for the oppressed, a refuge in times of trouble.* [The Lord has established his throne for judgment. He will judge the world in righteousness. He will govern the people with justice.]

Pray: God! You are a refuge for those who haven't been treated fairly in our justice system. You're a protector for those who have been wrongly charged or incarcerated. Father, come to their rescue, in Jesus' name! Judge those who have judged wrongly. Convict and correct them and let the innocent be free, in Jesus' name!

Psalm 9:16: *The Lord is known by the judgment which he executeth: the wicked is snared in the work of his own hands.* [The Lord is known by His justice; the wicked are ensnared by the works of His hands.]

Pray: Oh Father, I agree with Your Word! The wicked shall be snared in his own trap! In Jesus' name!

Psalm 11:7: *For the righteous Lord loveth righteousness; his countenance doth behold the upright.* [For the Lord is righteous; He loves justice.]

Pray: God, I am praying from this book because I know You love righteousness and justice. And I know this nation was founded on those principles, but we've strayed quite far from them. Father, turn us back to You! Turn us back to honesty and truth and fairness! Turn us back to right living and faith, hope, and love, in Jesus' name!

Psalm 33:5: *He loveth righteousness and judgment [justice]: the earth is full of the goodness of the Lord.*

Pray: The earth is full of Your goodness, God! Lately we hear a lot about evil things that are happening-human trafficking, bribery in high places, lies, perversion, and addictions- at every level of society. Father, I choose to look on Your goodness and focus on Your strength. Bring revival to this nation so people turn from their wicked ways and turn to You, in Jesus' name!

Psalm 37:5-6: *Commit thy way unto the Lord; trust also in him; and he shall bring it to pass. And he shall bring forth thy righteousness as the light, and thy judgment* [justice] *as the noonday.*

Pray: Father, I'm sorry that I've allowed myself to worry about what's happening in our nation. Today I decide to trust in You! I trust, rely, depend on You, God, even when things are bleak, and it looks like the world is going to hell in a handbasket! My eyes are on You. Bring forth Your righteousness and light in this very dark time, in Jesus' name!

Psalm 37:8-9: *Cease from anger and forsake wrath: fret not thyself in any wise to do evil.* [Do not fret; it leads only to evil] *For evildoers shall be cut off: but those that wait upon the Lord, they shall inherit the earth.* [Evil people will be cut off, but those who hope in the Lord will inherit the land.]

Pray: Well, here's that worry issue again! Worry doesn't produce anything good, does it, Lord? Worry is faith in the devil, and I don't want to have faith in him. I put my faith in You, Lord. Your Word says *evil people will be cut off,* so I agree with Your Word. Cut off the evil from positions of power and authority and let those with good and righteous hearts inherit the land. Let Your people increase in wealth while the evil ones lose their influence, in Jesus' name!

Psalm 37:10: *For yet a little while, and the wicked shall not be: yea, thou shalt diligently consider his place, and it shall not be.*

[A little while, and the wicked will be no more; though you look for them, they will not be found.]

Pray: Okay, God! You said it! You said the wicked would come to an end. I'm asking You make it happen now for us in this nation, in Jesus' name.

Psalm 37:12-13: *The wicked plotteth against the just, and gnasheth upon him with his teeth. The Lord shall laugh at him: for he seeth that his day is coming.* [The Lord laughs at the wicked, for He knows their day is coming.]

Pray: Ha-Ha-Ha-Ha. I laugh with You, Lord, at the wicked. They try to frighten us, but You sit on Your throne and laugh at them! The devil thinks he's won, Ha-Ha-Ha! The enemy says we'll never get out of this mess! Ha-Ha-Ha! When they crucified Jesus, the Romans and the Jewish nonbelievers all scoffed at Him, but He had the last laugh, didn't He, Lord? And so do we! God, You win and we are on the winning side! Praise the Lord! Ha-Ha-Ha!

Psalm 45:6-7: *Thy throne, O God, is for ever and ever: the sceptre of thy kingdom is a right sceptre.* [Your throne, O God, will last forever and ever; a scepter of justice will be the scepter of Your kingdom.] *Thou lovest righteousness, and hatest wickedness: therefore God, thy God, hath anointed thee with the oil of gladness above thy fellows.*

Pray: Father, Your throne lasts forever, but every elected official, monarch, or bureaucrat will soon topple off theirs. In the name of Jesus, I will not be impressed with them as they act as if they have complete authority over my life. My life belongs to You, God and knowing that anoints me with the oil of joy! Thank You,

God for always reigning on Your throne and for always hearing my prayers, in Jesus' name!

Psalm 72:1-2: *Give the king thy judgments, O God, and thy righteousness unto the king's son. He shall judge thy people with righteousness, and thy poor with judgment.* [Endow the king with justice, O God. Then, he will judge Your people in righteousness and Your afflicted ones with justice.]

Pray: Give our leaders wisdom, O God! Give our Senators wisdom, O God! Give our Congresspeople wisdom, O God! Give our Judges wisdom, O God! Give our President and Vice President wisdom, O God! They may not even be godly people, but I'm asking that You send laborers across their paths to tell them about You. If they refuse to hear and respond to You, I ask that You remove them so Your afflicted ones will experience justice, in Jesus' name.

Psalm 89:14: *Justice and judgment are the habitation of thy throne: mercy and truth shall go before thy face.* [Righteousness and justice are the foundation of God's throne.]

Pray: Father, righteousness and justice are the foundation of Your throne, so I ask that You move on this earth to establish righteousness and justice in our nation, in Jesus' name.

Psalm 97:1-2: *The Lord reigneth; let the earth rejoice; let the multitude of isles be glad thereof. Clouds and darkness are round about him: righteousness and judgment* [judgment] *are the habitation of his throne.*

Pray: God, You reign! Reign, Lord, over our seats of government! Reign, Lord, over our economy! Reign, Lord, over our schools, colleges, and universities! Reign, Lord, over our churches! Reign, Lord, over my life, in Jesus' name.

Psalm 99:4: *The king's strength also loveth judgment; thou dost establish equity, thou executest judgment and righteousness in Jacob.* [The king is mighty; He loves justice. You have established equity; in Jacob You have done what is just and right.]

Pray: God, You are mighty! Regardless of who or what is trying to do wrong, You always do right. Have Your way in our land, in Jesus' name!

Psalm 101:1: *I will sing of mercy and judgment* [justice]*: unto thee, O Lord, will I sing.*

Pray: Well, Lord, I'm going to do *Psalm 101:1;* I'm going to sing of mercy and judgment. I don't care who hears me or whether they like my singing. I'm singing it to You! You are worthy of all praise, honor, and adoration! (*Sing a song about the goodness of God!*)

Psalm 103:6: *The Lord executeth righteousness and judgment* [justice] *for all that are oppressed.*

Pray: Father, so many are oppressed today. So many have suffered at the hands of evil men and women in so many ways. Many have been oppressed by addiction, sexual perversion and sin and I lift up those whose lives, families and futures have been nearly destroyed by evil plots and ploys against them. I declare the devil will not win. Jesus died to set them free! God, send a laborer to them and open their hearts to receive complete freedom from all oppression, in Jesus' name!

Psalm 106:3: *Blessed are they that keep judgment, and he that doeth righteousness at all times.* [Blessed are they who maintain justice, who constantly do what is right.]

Pray: God, we bless those who maintain justice and who do what's right even though they may stand alone. I ask that You increase the numbers of people in my city, state, and nation who act justly and constantly do what's right. Help me to always do what's right, in Jesus' name.

Psalm 112:5-6: *A good man sheweth favour, and lendeth: he will guide his affairs with discretion.* [Good will come to him who is generous and lends freely who conducts his affairs with justice.] *Surely he shall not be moved for ever: the righteous shall be in everlasting remembrance.* [Surely he will never be shaken; a righteous man will be remembered forever.]

Pray: Father, thank You for good men and women who conduct their affairs with justice. When I vote for people, show me who is a good person who will conduct the affairs of government with justice. Alert more people to who is conducting themselves properly and who is not. Father, I ask that Your people, in particular, would stop voting for people who say they're Christians, but they don't legislate like they are. We need good people in government who will be generous, honest, and fair, in Jesus' name.

Psalm 140:12: *I know that the Lord will maintain the cause of the afflicted, and the right of the poor.* [I know that the Lord secures justice for the poor and upholds the cause of the needy.]

Pray: Oh Father, the poor and needy have always faced an uphill battle but Jesus came to preach the Gospel to the poor; He came *to heal the brokenhearted, to preach deliverance to the captives, and recovering of sight to the blind, to set at liberty them that are bruised. (Luke 4:18)* God, I am willing to give and be a blessing to those in need. Show me where and how to share with them. Most of all, I am willing to share the Gospel with them, so they don't have to be poor anymore. Father, I ask that You improve the quality of public defenders for the poor. Make them passionate about securing justice for those who aren't wealthy. If men or women are incarcerated unjustly because they couldn't afford an excellent lawyer, make it right, Lord! Set them free, in Jesus' name!

Proverbs 8:20: *I lead in the way of righteousness, in the midst of the paths of judgment.* [I, wisdom, walk in the way of righteousness, along the paths of justice.]

Pray: Lord, wisdom is in the paths of justice. I ask that You increase our wisdom so we can discern justice, in Jesus' name.

Proverbs 16:10: *A divine sentence is in the lips of the king: his mouth transgresseth not in judgment.* [The lips of a king speak as an oracle, and his mouth should not betray justice.]

Pray: Oh, Lord! How many people allow their lips to betray justice? I've heard people say, *"loose lips sink ships."* I know it's not in the Bible, but Your Word says we are *snared by the words of our mouth! (Proverbs 6:2)* I repent for saying things that weren't true or accurate. Please forgive me for spouting my opinion when I should have shared Your Word.

Proverbs 17:23: *A wicked man taketh a gift out of the bosom to pervert the ways of judgment.* [A wicked man accepts a bribe in secret to pervert the course of justice.]

Pray: Father, reveal those in authority who are taking bribes. Make it absolutely obvious who is governing based on who will pay them or reward them for decisions and choices and put a stop to it, in Jesus' name.

Proverbs 18:5: *It is not good to accept the person of the wicked, to overthrow the righteous in judgment.* [It is not good to be partial to the wicked or to deprive the innocent of justice.]

Pray: Father, in Jesus' name, I ask that You overthrow the wicked and that the wicked will not overthrow the innocent! Overthrow the wicked, Father, to Your glory, in Jesus' name!

Proverbs 19:28: *An ungodly witness scorneth judgment: and the mouth of the wicked devoureth iniquity.* [A corrupt witness mocks at justice, and the mouth of the wicked gulps down evil.]

Pray: Father, You know and I know people put their right hand up, swearing they will tell the truth on the witness stand, but they don't. Some of them are bought off. Others are trying to protect themselves. Still others have no regard for truth. Father, I ask that You inspire legal counsel to do better at uncovering lies in court and give judges discernment to do the same, in Jesus' name.

Proverbs 21:15: *It is joy to the just to do judgment: but destruction shall be to the workers of iniquity.* [When justice is done, it brings joy to the righteous but terror to evildoers!]

Pray: Father, justice brings joy to Your people, but terror to those who oppose You and Your ways. It seems like evildoers have not been terrified recently; they've been emboldened! We cry out for justice, Father, in Jesus' name.

Proverbs 28:5: *Evil men understand not judgment: but they that seek the Lord understand all things.* [Evil men do not understand justice, but those who seek the Lord understand it fully.]

Pray: God, I am seeking You and want to understand justice. Right now, it seems like justice has two levels. Some people do terrible things and aren't even charged. Others have done minor infractions and are serving years in jail. Father, I don't know what to do about this, but I know to pray. I know to seek Your face and ask You to intervene. So, Father, begin to move things in our society so justice is served, in Jesus' name.

Proverbs 29:4: *The king by judgment establisheth the land: but he that receiveth gifts overthroweth it.* [By justice, a king gives a country stability, but for one who is greedy for bribes tears it down.]

Pray: Lord, our country is not stable because justice is not being served in many cases. Father, please move people, change things, and open eyes to inequities in our judicial system. Give us elected officials that love and operate in justice so our country will be stable. In Jesus' name.

Proverbs 29:7: *The righteous considereth the cause of the poor: but the wicked regardeth not to know it.* [The righteous care about justice for the poor, but the wicked have no such concern.]

Pray: Father, as one of Your people, I care about justice for the poor, but it seems the wicked, who don't, are in many positions of power in our nation. God, start removing those wicked people and put the righteous in their place, who will see that the poor get justice, in Jesus' name.

Proverbs 29:26-27: *Many seek the ruler's favour; but every man's judgment cometh from the Lord.* [Many seek an audience with a ruler, but it is from the Lord that man gets justice.] *An unjust man is an abomination to the just: and he that is upright in the way is abomination to the wicked.*

Pray: Father, I believe You can give me favor with important people, and I am grateful for that! I look forward to influencing people of influence. I look forward to praying with government officials and business leaders, but I am most grateful that even before I know any movers and shakers in this world; I know You! I'd rather have one moment of favor with You than years of favor with any person. So, I ask You, Lord, to bring justice to this nation. Do away with different levels of justice based on who a person is, how much they're worth or who they know, in Jesus' name!

Ecclesiastes 3:16-17: *And moreover I saw under the sun the place of judgment, that wickedness was there; and the place of righteousness, that iniquity was there.* [Wickedness was there in the place of judgment.] *I said in mine heart, God shall judge the*

righteous and the wicked: for there is a time there for every
purpose and for every work.

Pray: Father, I agree with Your Word! You shall judge the
righteous and the wicked! There is a time for every purpose and
for every work, so I won't worry about the timing. I'll only believe
what You said shall come to pass, in Jesus' name!

Ecclesiastes 5:8-9: *If thou seest the oppression of the poor,*
and violent perverting of judgment and justice in a province,
marvel not at the matter: for he that is higher than the highest
regardeth; and there be higher than they. Moreover the profit of
the earth is for all: the king himself is served by the field. [If you
see the poor oppressed in a district and justice and rights denied,
do not be surprised at such things. For one official is eyed by a
higher one, and over them both are others still. The increase from
the land is taken by all; the kin himself profits from the fields.]

Pray: O my! Lord, You told me not to be surprised at
injustice! Father, my prayer is that I and others who are honest
and fair would not lose heart when we see the number of
injustices in our nation. I will not be weary in praying and
believing, for I believe our prayers make a difference, in Jesus'
name.

Isaiah 1:17: *Learn to do well; seek judgment, relieve the*
oppressed, judge the fatherless, plead for the widow. [Stop doing
wrong! Learn to do right. Seek justice; encourage the oppressed!]

Pray: Lord, teach me to do right, to seek justice and to
encourage the oppressed. I think I'm on the right track, but if not,
I'm listening and I will receive Your correction so I can be a

blessing to the world and an excellent representative of Your Kingdom, in Jesus' name!

Isaiah 1:21: *How is the faithful city become an harlot! it was full of judgment; righteousness lodged in it; but now murderers.* [The faithful city has become a harlot. She once was full of justice; righteousness used to dwell in her-but now, murderers!]

Pray: Oh Father, have mercy on this nation that was once known as a Judeo-Christian stronghold. We've striven to be a nation of justice but have fallen short so many times. Yet now it seems people are easily and often bought. They trade principles for power, guts for gold, and decency for degradation. I repent on behalf of my nation, but I know, Lord, there are many righteous in this nation who still believe You. You said You would spare Sodom and Gomorrah if You could find ten righteous there. Oh, God, I ask that You spare this nation for the sake of Your righteous ones who call You their Lord, in Jesus' name.

Isaiah 1:23: *Thy princes are rebellious, and companions of thieves: every one loveth gifts, and followeth after rewards: they judge not the fatherless, neither doth the cause of the widow come unto them.* [Your rulers are rebels, companions of thieves; they all love bribes and chase after gifts.]

Pray: God, I don't know how many of our government officials are companions of thieves, but You do. So, Father, I ask that You root them out. Convict them and bring laborers across their paths who can effectively share the Gospel with them. In Jesus' name.

Isaiah 1:26: *And I will restore thy judges as at the first, and thy counsellors as at the beginning: afterward thou shalt be called, The city of righteousness, the faithful city.*

Pray: Father, I pray in agreement with Your Word. I ask You to restore our judges as You intend them to be: godly, honest, fair, righteous, and merciful. Remove judges who make decisions based on political positions or who have been bought, in Jesus' name.

Isaiah 5:7: *For the vineyard of the Lord of hosts is the house of Israel, and the men of Judah his pleasant plant: and he looked for judgment* [justice], *but behold oppression; for righteousness, but behold a cry.* [God looked for justice but saw bloodshed; for righteousness, but heard cries of distress.]

Pray: Father, You established Israel because of Your love for Your people. How it must have grieved You when the men of Judah chose oppression over righteousness. America was established not because of Your love for it, but because the people who founded it loved You. Hear our cries of distress, Oh Lord! Hear our cries for freedom, justice, peace, and prosperity. Hear our cry, O God and clean our government from top to bottom. Clean my home and heart, too, Lord, so that my life represents You well, in Jesus' name.

Isaiah 5:22-23: *Woe unto them that are mighty to drink wine, and men of strength to mingle strong drink: Which justify the wicked for reward, and take away the righteousness of the righteous from him!* [Woe to those who are heroes at drinking wine and champions at mixing drinks, who acquit the guilty for a bribe, but deny justice to the innocent.]

Pray: Lord, we have a lot of people in our nation that are professionals at drinking wine, beer, and every other kind of spirit. They do it as if it were a job-sometimes drinking five or six hours a day. They think they're functioning well, but their senses are numbed and so are their souls. Some of them do it because they have nothing else that brings them joy. Lord, I pray for those whose hearts are so dissipated that they can only be happy when they're under the influence. Send someone to them who can give them genuine hope by introducing them to You and Your Son, Jesus. I pray specifically for anyone I know personally who is addicted to drugs, booze, or sex. I break that demonic power that is holding them to the addiction. I command those demons to leave my loved one alone. Loose them and let them go, in Jesus' name. And Father, I pray that those who are entrusted with making decisions for others would not be under the influence of any spirit but Yours, in Jesus' name.

Isaiah 9:7: *Of the increase of his government and peace there shall be no end, upon the throne of David, and upon his kingdom, to order it, and to establish it with judgment and with justice from henceforth even for ever. The zeal of the Lord of hosts will perform this.*

Pray: Father, You told us through Isaiah the Prophet that Messiah would bring a kingdom of justice. Lord, I know this is talking about the millennial reign, but I also know that where Jesus is allowed to reign today, He brings judgment and justice with Him. Our problem is that our government has cut You out-almost completely so there is little justice and much injustice. Your justice brings peace, but what many District Attorneys call justice today is not bringing peace; their decisions allow rioting, burning, looting, and violent attacks on innocent people. Their idea of justice is releasing anyone who has had to deal with poverty, racism, or other issues beyond their control. Some assault or even kill others and serve little or no jail time. For years, much of the justice system was skewed completely the opposite way and any person of color or low income was immediately judged guilty and sent to jail for ridiculously long sentences. But this overcorrection isn't helping raise people out of poverty or equal the playing field in America. Their version of justice is not bringing peace; it is making our cities dangerous. Father, remove D.A.s, Attorneys General and Law Enforcement Officers who refuse to honestly follow the law. Fill their positions with people who have Your wisdom, who have mercy but will also enforce the law so our cities will be peaceful again, in Jesus' name.

Isaiah 51:5: *My righteousness is near; my salvation is gone forth, and mine arms shall judge the people; the isles shall wait upon me, and on mine arm shall they trust.* [My righteousness draws near speedily; my salvation is on the way, and my arm will bring justice to the nations.]

Pray: Father, You've already sent righteousness and salvation in Your Son, Jesus. But Father, many or most of the people with power in our nation give Jesus lip-service if they do anything positive about Him at all. They say they're Christians, and Father, only You know their hearts, but You told us we would know them by their fruits. *(Matthew 7:16;20)* When people say they belong to a large denomination, but they support allowing a

71

baby who survived abortion to be left to die, their fruit tells me they don't know You. We command the blinders come off their eyes so they can see the true state of their hearts. Send laborers across their paths, Lord, who can share the Good News of the Gospel with power and let Your goodness and lead them to repentance, in Jesus' name.

Isaiah 56:1: *Thus saith the Lord, Keep ye judgment, and do justice: for my salvation is near to come, and my righteousness to be revealed.* [Maintain justice and do what is right, for my salvation is close at hand and my righteousness will soon be revealed.]

Pray: Dear God, help me do what is right and to maintain justice. Show me issues where I have not judged fairly or have taken the wrong side. I humble myself to admit I don't know everything, and I am willing to change. Your salvation has come in Jesus Christ, my Lord, and Your righteousness was revealed in Him. But God, I want to see more righteousness revealed in our city, state, and nation. Please show me what I can do to establish or maintain justice to Your glory, in Jesus' name.

Isaiah 58:6: *Is not this the fast that I have chosen? to loose the bands of wickedness,* [injustice] *to undo the heavy burdens, and to let the oppressed go free, and that ye break every yoke?*

Pray: Oh Lord! So many people do things to look holy, but their hearts are far from You. They do nothing to undo others' burdens. On the contrary, they often put more encumbrances on people in the form of taxes, restrictive laws, and censorship while they spout their so-called "good works" protecting animals' rights above babies' rights or violently protesting Christians who preach Your Word. God, I choose Your kind of fast. Help me fight injustice and lift burdens and yokes from people. Help me rescue men and women from addictions and the control of dealers, traffickers, and others who exist to keep people in bondage. God, I want to really be holy, not just look holy. I want to please You, in Jesus' name.

Isaiah 59:1-3: *Behold, the Lord's hand is not shortened, that it cannot save; neither his ear heavy, that it cannot hear: But your iniquities have separated between you and your God, and your sins have hid his face from you, that he will not hear. For your hands are defiled with blood, and your fingers with iniquity; your lips have spoken lies, your tongue hath muttered perverseness.*

Pray: Oh God, You have not changed! You are the same God who created heaven and earth and everything on it. You are the same God who brought Your people out of Egypt and split the Red Sea to set them free. You are the same God who has provided abundance to Your servants in famines. You've healed the incurably ill and You've raised the dead. Your arm is not shortened, and Your ear is not deaf to my cry. God, we find ourselves in a mess in our nation and it seems like You've left us, but *Isaiah 59:1-3* tells us why. We have shed innocent blood, aborting 63 million babies. Our hands have been busy, not doing Your work, but indulging our lusts; most people today don't give a second thought about lying, and perverse conversations, pictures, and videos run rampant. Father, I cry for Your mercy upon our nation. I pray for people to turn to You. You said, *"If My people, who are called by My name would humble themselves and pray, and seek my face, and turn from their wicked ways, THEN you*

*would hear from heaven, forgive their sins and HEAL THEIR LAND."
(2 Chronicles 7:14)* Father, I'm doing that and I'm praying others will too. I'm committed to encouraging others to do *2 Chronicles 7:14* too. God, I pray our nation would turn from its wicked ways and would seek Your face. I ask that You hear and save us from the natural result of decades of sinful living, in the powerful, mighty name of Jesus!

Isaiah 59:4: *None calleth for justice, nor any pleadeth for truth: they trust in vanity, and speak lies; they conceive mischief, and bring forth iniquity.*

Pray: God, I am one who calls for justice! I call for it now! I do not trust in empty arguments or what "everyone" says. I trust in Your Word. If I must stand alone on Your Word, I will. But I believe You are raising an army of honest, righteous people who want to do right and who know You are the only source of righteousness. You are the source of freedom and justice. You are the source of honesty, and Your Word is truth. Lord, it seems like none call for justice, but I know there are some. Please lead me to them so we can work together to do Your will, in Jesus' matchless name!

Isaiah 59:8: *The way of peace they know not; and there is no judgment in their goings: they have made them crooked paths: whosoever goeth therein shall not know peace.* [The way of peace, they do not know. There is no justice in their paths. They have turned them into crooked roads. No one who walks in them will have peace.]

Pray: Jehovah Shalom! You are the Lord my Peace! But so many people don't know You, and since they don't know the Prince of Peace, they don't know the way of peace. They seek the easy way, which is often not Your way. They follow paths created by ideologues and then get frustrated when those roads lead to sickness, depression, addiction, strife, anger, hatred, and pain. Help me speak peace and reveal You as Jehovah Shalom to the many people I interact with who do not know You, in the name of the Prince of Peace, Jesus Christ, our Lord.

Jeremiah 23:5: *Behold, the days come, saith the Lord, that I will raise unto David a righteous Branch, and a King shall reign and prosper, and shall execute judgment and justice in the earth.*

Pray: Jesus, You are Lord! You are David's righteous branch. You came the first time over 2,000 years ago to establish Your Kingdom in the hearts of those who believe in You. But the day is coming, and I think it may be soon, when You are coming back in Your glorified, undefeatable body, to execute judgment and justice on the earth. I'm ready, Lord, but I know many are not. Please do whatever You need to do to open their eyes. Wake them out of their spiritual stupor. We live in unprecedented times. *Revelation 12:12* reveals why evil is at such a fevered pitch these days. It says, *Woe to the inhabiters of the earth and of the sea! for the devil is come down unto you, having great wrath, because he knoweth that he hath but a short time.* The devil is running out of time, and he is doing everything he can to take as many people to hell with him as he can. Lord, help me reach more people with the Truth so they can reign with You and prosper and not suffer the consequences of Your justice and judgment for those who do evil, in the name of Jesus.

Ezekiel 45:9: *Thus saith the Lord God; Let it suffice you, O princes of Israel: remove violence and spoil, and execute judgment and justice, take away your exactions from my people, saith the Lord God.*

Pray: El Elyon, the God of all gods, You spoke through the prophet Ezekiel and told the princes of Israel You had enough! It was time for them to stop abusing their authority. So, God, we pray that those in our nation who are abusing their authority will hit the wall of Your displeasure and stop their draconian ways that limit our freedom, in Jesus' name.

Matthew 12:18-19: *Behold my servant, whom I have chosen; my beloved, in whom my soul is well pleased: I will put my spirit upon him, and he shall shew judgment* [justice] *to the Gentiles. He shall not strive, nor cry; neither shall any man hear his voice in the streets.*

Pray: Father, for over 2,000 years, your chosen people were the Jews and only the Jews. Anyone who wasn't Jewish had no way of approaching You or receiving favorable judgment from You. But then You sent Jesus, and He made the way for every person from any nation, any color, and language, any tribe to *come boldly unto the throne of grace, that we may obtain mercy, and find grace to help in time of need. (Hebrews 4:16)* So, I approach boldly approach Your throne of grace. Our nation needs mercy. Forgive us for our sins of prioritizing everything above You. Forgive us for murdering innocent children in their mothers' wombs. Forgive us for esteeming opinions over Your Word. I am thankful to be able to talk to You, to seek Your face, and receive Your justice, in Jesus' name.

Matthew 23:23: *"Woe to you, teachers of the law and Pharisees, you hypocrites! You give a tenth of your spices—mint, dill and cumin. But you have neglected the more important matters of the law—justice, mercy and faithfulness. You should have practiced the latter, without neglecting the former.*

Pray: God, in the Old Covenant, You outlined 613 laws people had to follow to please You, but when Jesus came, He fulfilled all the law! Lord, I know that means I can't live any old way. I pay a tenth of my income, called a tithe, to my church because Jesus said it was still valid in the New Testament. But beyond that, Jesus said You required justice, mercy, and faithfulness. Help me live these values and show me how to influence those around me to do the same, in Jesus' name.

Luke 18:1-8: *And he spake a parable unto them to this end, that men ought always to pray, and not to faint; Saying, There was in a city a judge, which feared not God, neither regarded man: And there was a widow in that city; and she came unto him, saying, Avenge me of mine adversary. And he would not for a while: but afterward he said within himself, Though I fear not God, nor regard man; Yet because this widow troubleth me, I will avenge her, lest by her continual coming she weary me. And the Lord said, Hear what the unjust judge saith. And shall not God avenge his own elect, which cry day and night unto him, though he bear long with them? I tell you that he will avenge them speedily. Nevertheless when the Son of man cometh, shall he find faith on the earth?*

Pray: Oh, Father! This parable about the unjust judge is so timely! Some preachers say the unjust judge is You, but I know it's not because You are not unjust, and the judge in the parable didn't care about people. You are just and You care. I believe the unjust judge in the parable represents the devil, who has jurisdiction over the earth. *2 Corinthians 4:4* calls Satan the *god of this world.* You gave authority on this earth to humanity when You said, *Let us make man in our image, after our likeness: and let them have dominion over the fish of the sea, and over the fowl of the air, and over the cattle, and over all the earth, and over every creeping thing that creepeth upon the earth. (Genesis 1:26)* But when Adam bowed to the serpent, he became the servant of the evil one. *Romans 6:16* confirms, *Know ye not, that to whom ye yield yourselves servants to obey, his servants ye are to whom ye obey; whether of sin unto death, or of obedience unto righteousness?* So, I understand that our battle to see Your will done in our homes, businesses, schools, churches, and communities is against the unjust judge, the devil. *Ephesians 6:12* tells us our battle is not against people. It reads, *we wrestle not against flesh and blood, but against principalities, against powers, against the rulers of the darkness of this world, against spiritual wickedness in high places.* We've got unjust judges, legislators and others making decisions that hurt people, and I determine not to give the devil any peace. I will continually remind him, myself and everyone listening that Jesus is Lord and You are God. I command the devil to take his hands off me, my family, my city, state, and nation. I will not let up. I will praise Your name until the devil can't stand to listen to me anymore! I will remind him of his final demise, and of Jesus' eternal victory! Father, Jesus ended the parable with a question. He asked if He would find faith on the earth when He returns. Lord, that word for faith means *this kind of perseverant faith.* I will not give up! I will not give the devil any territory and I will pray and praise You until we take more territory from him. Father, help Your people to continue to believe, continue to pray, and continue to praise You even when the unjust judge influences earthly judges to do wrong. God, You are bigger than any judge. You are the eternal Judge and, in the end, You win! Hallelujah!

John 7:24: *Judge not according to the appearance, but judge righteous judgment.*

Pray: Lord, I'm sorry for the times I've judged by appearance. I know it's not right, but You and I both know just about everyone does it at times. Father, some say we shouldn't judge anyone...ever...at all...but that is not what Your Word says. Jesus told us to judge, but to judge righteously. Father, help me not to judge people based on their race, financial or marital status, or what church they attend. When Jesus talked about *righteous judgment,* I believe He meant we can and should judge actions, but we can't judge intentions. Father, Your Word tells us to choose godly associations. So, if we see immoral behavior or hear inappropriate language, we can judge their actions, but not their heart; we cannot judge their intentions. And God, I must admit, I've done that. I've assumed the worst about people, and I repent of that. Father, help our nation to learn to judge actions according to Your Word but not to judge intentions. You know people's hearts and You will judge them one day. Help me, Lord to make righteous judgments and I ask that others would stop making wrong judgments about me because I stand for You, in Jesus' name!

Acts 17: 30-31: *And the times of this ignorance God winked at; but now commandeth all men every where to repent: Because* *he hath appointed a day, in the which he will judge the world in righteousness by that man whom he hath ordained; whereof he hath given assurance unto all men, in that he hath raised him from the dead.*

Pray: WOAH! The day when You judge the world in righteousness is not far away, Lord! Although many people know something is happening, most don't think Jesus is coming back soon because it's been over 2,000 years! Thank You for Your Word that deals with everything we face today. Around 70 A.D., the Apostle Peter wrote, *Knowing this first, that there shall come in the last days scoffers, walking after their own lusts, and saying, Where is the promise of his coming? for since the fathers fell asleep, all things continue as they were from the beginning of the creation.* (2 Peter 3:3-4) God, I am NOT a scoffer. I believe Jesus is coming soon, but even if I'm wrong, our lives are very short, and the day of judgment is not far away for any of us. Help me live like You're coming back today. Help me tell people about You so they aren't on the wrong side on the day of judgment, in Jesus' name!

Revelation 6:9-11: *And when he had opened the fifth seal, I saw under the altar the souls of them that were slain for the word of God, and for the testimony which they held: And they cried with a loud voice, saying, How long, O Lord, holy and true, dost thou not judge and avenge our blood on them that dwell on the earth? And white robes were given unto every one of them; and it was said unto them, that they should rest yet for a little season, until their fellowservants also and their brethren, that should be killed as they were, should be fulfilled.*

Pray: Oh Father, people are being killed today for the Word of God. Persecution of Christians is worse now than it was in the first century. I'm not telling You anything You don't already know, but God, I repent for not praying for my Christian brothers and sisters living under persecution. In some countries, Christians are being tortured and killed. Churches are burned to the ground, and in America, radical groups are attacking Christian individuals and churches. Father, I pray Christians will not back up under persecution. I ask that You send angels to help them, protect them, and strengthen them. I pray governments will not treat Christians as criminals. Even our own government, Lord, has labeled pro-life activists and parents who speak out at School Board Meetings as terrorists. Some politicians who have stood up for Christian values have been unfairly targeted and prosecuted for things other politicians get away Father, bring a stop to this political persecution in the United States, in Jesus' name. Amen.

Revelation 11:18: *And the nations were angry, and thy wrath is come, and the time of the dead, that they should be judged, and that thou shouldest give reward unto thy servants the prophets, and to the saints, and them that fear thy name, small and great; and shouldest destroy them which destroy the earth.*

Pray: Hallelujah, Lord God! You reign! The time is coming when you will reward Your servants and judge the nations. Father, Your Word says at the end of days, You will judge some nations as goat nations and some as sheep nations. Sheep nations are those who stand with Israel, support Your people, and do Your will. Goat nations do not. Father, it seems like America goes back and forth. I pray now that America will be found to be a sheep nation at the end and will find favor and mercy from You. Wake voters up,

Lord! I ask that they stop electing people who refuse to bow to You, and end support for ungodly organizations, in Jesus' name.

Revelation 20:12-13: *And I saw the dead, small and great, stand before God; and the books were opened: and another book was opened, which is the book of life: and the dead were judged out of those things which were written in the books, according to their works. And the sea gave up the dead which were in it; and death and hell delivered up the dead which were in them: and they were judged every man according to their works.*

Pray: Father, this will happen. Every man will be judged according to their works. Those who have accepted Jesus will be judged and rewarded on what they've done for You. Those who have rejected Your Son will be judged to eternal death. O God, help me to function with a sense of urgency to share the Gospel with everyone. Eternity is real and after we die, it's too late to choose You. Open people's eyes, Lord, and soften their hearts, Holy Spirit, so they will receive Jesus, serve God, and spend eternity with You in Heaven.

PROLOGUE

1 Timothy 2:1-4 is a portion of Scripture that Christians often use to pray for government and elected officials. It says, *I exhort therefore, that, first of all, supplications, prayers, intercessions, and giving of thanks, be made for all men; For kings, and for all that are in authority; that we may lead a quiet and peaceable life in all godliness and honesty. For this is good and acceptable in the sight of God our Saviour; Who will have all men to be saved, and to come unto the knowledge of the truth.*

I've heard this prayed often by ministers who include the names of the President, Vice President, Speaker of the House, President of the Senate, Governor, and Supreme Court Justices. Sometimes they even mention minority leaders in Congress! They try to cover as many by name as possible. Their supplications are usually heartfelt, whether the praying person agrees with the elected official or not. However, they're often, *"bless them, Lord,"* type of prayers, and I don't think that was what Paul had in mind when he wrote these verses.

All that were in authority in the Apostle Paul's day were antagonistic to followers of The Way. Paul was beaten, imprisoned, and finally died a martyr's death under the emperor Nero. Nero was mentally unstable and horribly cruel to people of faith.

In 64 C.E., much of Rome was burned to the ground in a fire that lasted almost six days. Many historians think Nero may have been behind the destruction, saying the emperor played the fiddle while Rome burned. Other historians aren't sure if Nero was behind the fire, but Nero used the fire to go after Christians. He arrested Christians, putting them to death in the cruelest ways. They were covered in animals' skins, chained, and torn to death by dogs. Some were crucified and others were tied to posts and set on fire to illuminate the streets.

This is the governmental authority for whom Paul told Timothy and the church to pray. I believe modern Christians often miss the point of Paul's prayer for those in authority. I've heard them pray, *"O God, bless our President, Vice President, Congresspeople and Senators,"* but that's not how Paul said to pray. He said to pray for those in authority so Christians could *live a quiet and peaceable life in all godliness and honesty.*

We should pray that the government would retain our liberty so we can do what God wants us to do. Yes, we should pray that they come to know Jesus, but at some point, we should pray that those who have hardened their hearts to God will be removed from authority.

Compassionate, twenty-first Century Christians want to operate in the fruit of the Spirit, which is love, joy, peace, patience, kindness, goodness, faithfulness, and self-control. (*Galatians 5:22*) But we forget that God told the Prophet Jeremiah three times to stop praying for rebellious, antagonistic people who repeatedly refused to do right and obey His Word. You can read it in *Jeremiah 7:16, Jeremiah 11:14* and *Jeremiah 14:11* that says, *then said the Lord unto me, Pray not for this people for their good.*

So, it's not un-Christian to pray that ungodly leaders be removed. However, we should remember to pray for protection for Christian politicians, and those who are kindly disposed to good, moral citizens. Pray that no laws would be passed that restrict our freedom to serve God, go to church, pay our tithe, give offerings to the poor, and raise our children according to God's Word.

The battle is fierce. We must cling to God's Word. Remember *greater is He* [the Holy Spirit] *that is in you than he that is in the world. (1 John 4:4)* And whatever you do, don't give up. Don't stop praying. Your words have power. Use your words strategically and continually. The Bible mentions the power of words in several Scriptures. *Romans 10:9-10* says a person is eternally saved by believing in their hearts and confessing with their mouths, *"Jesus is the Son of God who died on the cross and rose from the dead."* The heart matters, but so do your words. *Mark 11:23-24* says you can tell things to move, and they will move. *Proverbs 6:2* says your words can entrap you or set you free.

Release God's Word in prayer regularly. Do it with faith, believing things are moving. You may not see an immediate shift, but when you release faith and God's Word, things happen in the unseen realm.

Keep praying. Make prayer a daily priority but continue to engage. *James 2:20* says, *faith without works is dead."* Don't stop acting civically; consider becoming a Precinct Committeeman, attend your District Meetings, work the polls during elections, and don't stop fighting for liberty and justice for all.

GLORIA BRINTNALL

A PRAYER TO ACCEPT JESUS

Father, I've heard about You from many people, but I admit I don't really know You. I admit I'm a sinner and I need You. Thank You for sending Your Son, Jesus, to die on the cross for my sins. I believe He paid for my sins with His blood. He died and was buried, but on the third day, He rose from the dead, defeating death forever.

Jesus, come into my heart. I give You my life and I ask that You make something wonderful of it. Help me do Your will, to stand strong for what's right and to tell others about You.

I'm thankful to be a child of God now. Help me find a good church, Lord, where I can grow in wisdom and understanding of Your Word. Direct my steps so I can make a positive difference in this dark world. Jesus, You are the light of the world and I want You to shine through me. Thank You, Father, in Jesus' name!

GLORIA BRINTNALL

ABOUT THE AUTHOR

Gloria's book, *Stuff Happens, H.O.P.E. Anyway* was a #1 New Release on Amazon. She often speaks for women's groups, churches, and community organizations, sharing a message of faith, hope, and love. She works full-time as a ghostwriter, mostly for Christian organizations.

Gloria was first elected as a Precinct Committeeman in 1988, and after moving around the nation for over 20 years, has once again engaged in her community as an elected Precinct Committeeman and a State Committeeman for her Legislative District in the great state of Arizona.

A graduate of Arizona State University and Word of Faith Bible Training Center in Southfield, Michigan, Gloria has worked as an entrepreneur and minister, serving as a worship leader, Bible school instructor, staff minister, itinerant preacher, church planter, and pastor.

Gloria and her husband, the Amazing Mr. Mike Brintnall, U.S.M.C, have been married over ten years. Together, they have 6 children, 9 grandchildren, three old cars, and a lot of laughs.

GLORIA BRINTNALL

GLORIA BRINTNALL

Made in the USA
Las Vegas, NV
12 May 2023

71946642R00056